Explore Space Stations

Megan Harder

Lerner Publications ◆ Minneapolis

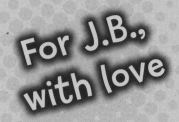

For J.B., with love

Lerner Publications Company
An imprint of Lerner Publishing Group, Inc.
241 First Avenue North
Minneapolis, MN 55401 USA

For reading levels and more information, look up this title at www.lernerbooks.com.

Main body text set in Billy Infant Regular. Typeface provided by SparkType.

Library of Congress Cataloging-in-Publication Data

Names: Harder, Megan, author.
Title: Explore space stations / Megan Harder.
Description: Minneapolis, MN: Lerner Publications Company, an imprint of Lerner Publishing Group, Inc., [2023] | Series: Lightning Bolt Books. Exploring space | Includes bibliographical references and index. | Audience: Ages 6–9. | Audience: Grades 2–3. | Summary: "Astronauts live and study on space stations. Readers will love learning fascinating details about these structures, from their beginnings to how they might be used in the future"—Provided by publisher.
Identifiers: LCCN 2021043611 (print) | LCCN 2021043612 (ebook) | ISBN 9781728457819 (lib. bdg.) | ISBN 9781728463483 (pbk.) | ISBN 9781728461601 (eb pdf)
Subjects: LCSH: Space stations—Juvenile literature.
Classification: LCC TL797.15 .H37 2023 (print) | LCC TL797.15 (ebook) | DDC 629.44/2—dc23/eng/20211108

LC record available at https://lccn.loc.gov/2021043611
LC ebook record available at https://lccn.loc.gov/2021043612

Manufactured in the United States of America
1-50809-50148-3/14/2022

Table of Contents

Home Away from Earth

A speck of light moves across the night sky. Is it an airplane? A shooting star? It might be a space station!

Space stations are homes and labs for astronauts in space. They can be used to do experiments or observe Earth. Future space stations could be stepping-stones to other planets.

Someday space stations may help astronauts see other planets up close.

The Story of Space Stations

A rocket roared as it left Earth in 1971. High above Earth, the rocket released the world's first space station. Its name was Salyut 1.

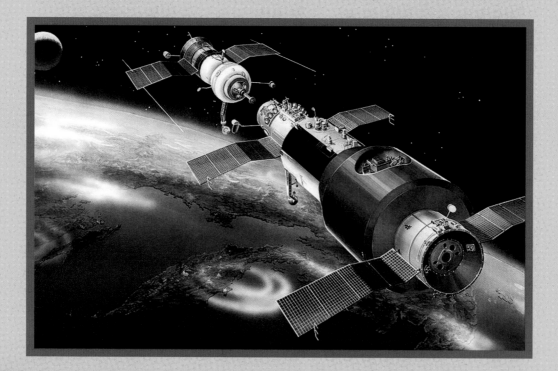

Skylab was America's first space station.

Early space stations were built on Earth. Then rockets launched them into space. Some were built for spying. Others were used for science missions.

Mir launched in 1986. At first, it looked like older stations. Then it started growing. One by one, sections called modules were added to Mir in space.

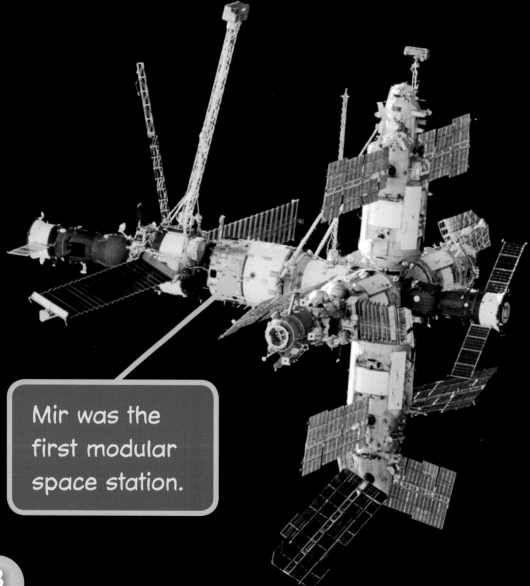

Mir was the first modular space station.

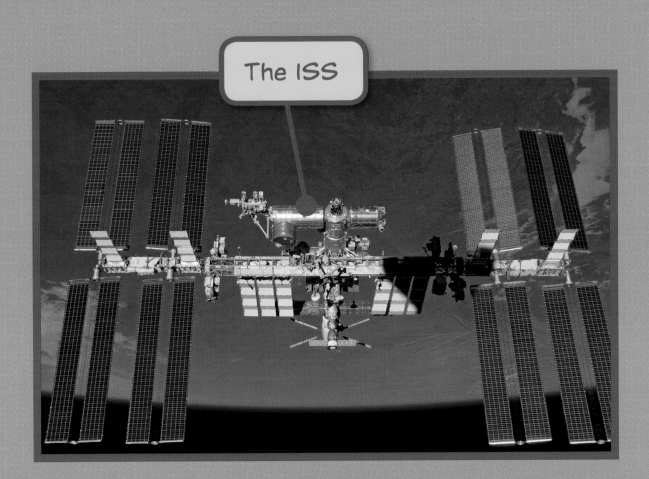

The ISS

In 1998, the US and Russia started something amazing. Together, they began building the International Space Station (ISS). Since then, people from around the world have worked together on the ISS.

Space Stations in Action

Space stations are busy places. Science is in action inside and outside the ISS!

The ISS is always moving. It makes loops around Earth. This is called orbiting. It can orbit Earth in just ninety minutes.

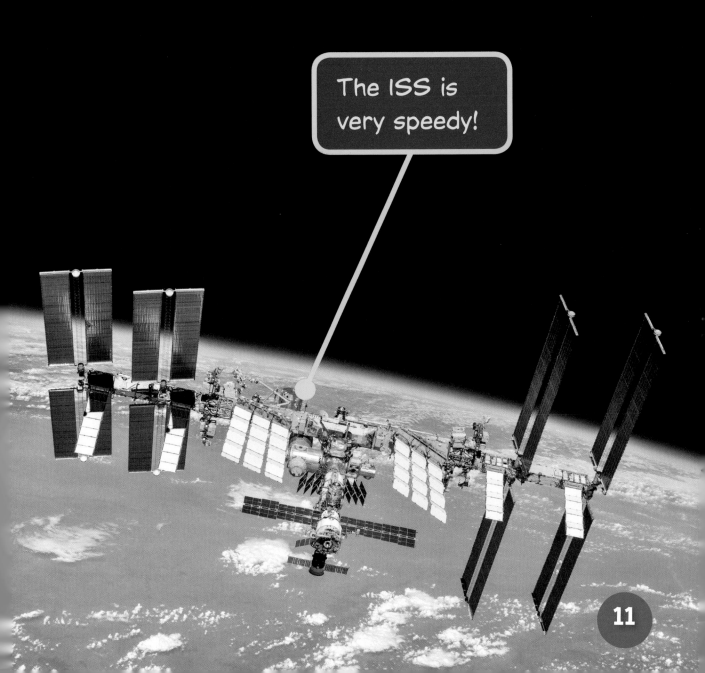

The ISS is very speedy!

Solar arrays stick out from the ISS. They catch sunlight and turn it into electricity. This power is used to run the station's many machines.

Solar array

The ISS-CREAM detects cosmic rays.

The outside of the ISS has equipment for observing Earth and space. Some of it looks for changes to Earth's air, water, plants, and weather.

Inside the station, people and things float! This is due to microgravity. In microgravity, astronauts can do experiments that are impossible on Earth.

Even the people on the ISS are an experiment. We still don't know all the ways that spaceflight can change people's bodies. Astronauts measure and record how their bodies act in space.

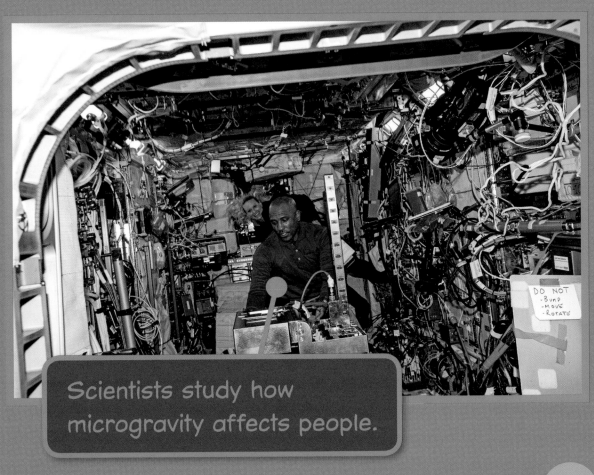

Scientists study how microgravity affects people.

DO NOT
- BUMP
- MOVE
- ROTATE

Into the Unknown

New space stations will build on the work of the ISS. Some will go where no space station has gone before.

Maybe someday space stations will go to Mars!

Tiangong

In 2021, China launched the first part of its new modular station, Tiangong. More than one thousand experiments are planned for Tiangong.

A NASA image of the Gateway

The first space station to orbit the moon will be called the Gateway. Later, Gateway could become a waypoint on the path to Mars.

One day, space stations could be like train stations. People might stop at a station on their way to other worlds. Would *you* like to travel through space?

Which planet would you like to visit?

Space Station Diagram

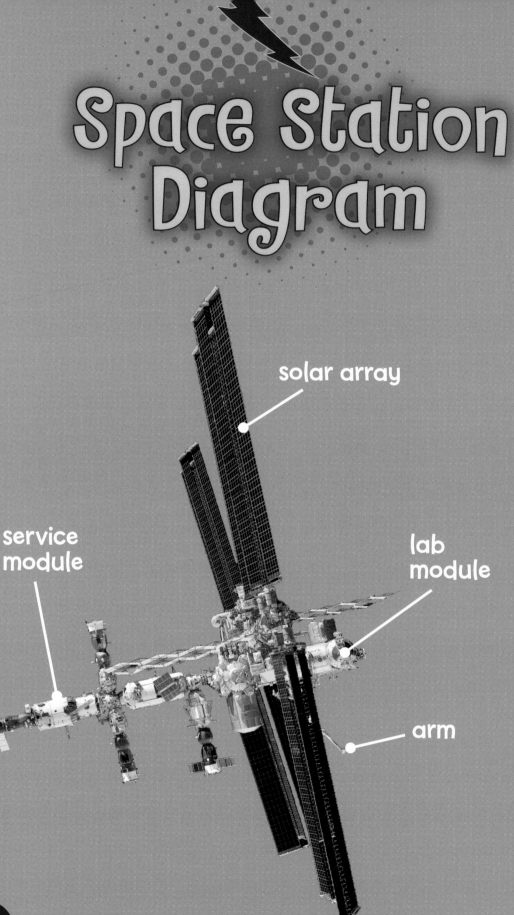

solar array

service module

lab module

arm

The Amazing Canadarm2

Did you know the ISS has arms? Canadarm2 is one of them. The robotic arm has two hands—one on each end. It uses its hands to "walk" to different areas on the outside of the station. People on Earth or astronauts in the ISS control the arm. They use Canadarm2 to catch spacecraft arriving from Earth. The arm is also used to fix broken parts on the station.

Glossary

astronaut: a person who is trained to work in outer space

electricity: energy released by flowing electrons

experiment: a test done by scientists to find out how something works

lab: a place to do science experiments. *Lab* is short for *laboratory*.

module: a part of a spacecraft that can be combined with others to create a larger whole

observe: to watch

orbit: to move around an object in space

solar array: a group of solar panels that turn energy from sunlight into electrical power

waypoint: a place to stop along a path

Learn More

Britannica Kids: Space Station
https://kids.britannica.com/kids/article/space
-station/390976

How Things Fly: Gravity in Orbit
https://howthingsfly.si.edu/flight-dynamics
/gravity-orbit

Kruesi, Liz. *Space.* Mankato, MN: Child's World, 2021.

Murray, Julie. *International Space Station.*
Minneapolis: Abdo Zoom, 2019.

NASA: International Space Station Tour
https://www.nasa.gov/mission_pages/station
/main/suni_iss_tour.html

Schaefer, Lola. *Explore Satellites.* Minneapolis:
Lerner Publications, 2023.

Index

Photo Acknowledgments

Image credits: Mohamad Noorashid/EyeEm/Getty Images, p. 4; NASA, pp. 5, 7, 8, 9, 10, 11, 13, 14, 15; Image courtesy of RIA-Novosti via NASA, p. 6; ESA/NASA, p. 12; NASA/JPL-Caltech/ USGS, p. 16; alejomiranda/Getty Images, p. 17; Credit: NASA/Alberto Bertolin, p. 18; m-gucci/ Getty Images, p. 19; NASA, p. 20.